CODING IS EVERYWHERE

Coding in Your School

by Elizabeth Noll

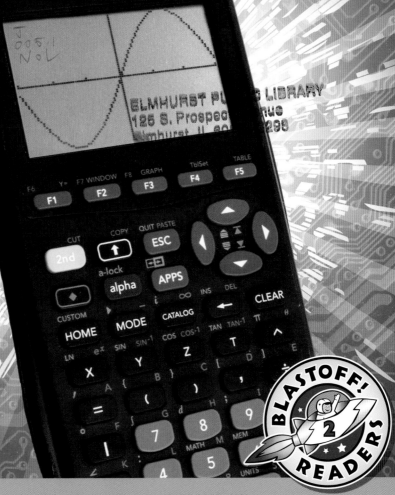

BELLWETHER MEDIA • MINNEAPOLIS, MN

Note to Librarians, Teachers, and Parents:

Blastoff! Readers are carefully developed by literacy experts and combine standards-based content with developmentally appropriate text.

Level 1 provides the most support through repetition of high-frequency words, light text, predictable sentence patterns, and strong visual support.

Level 2 offers early readers a bit more challenge through varied simple sentences, increased text load, and less repetition of high-frequency words.

Level 3 advances early-fluent readers toward fluency through increased text and concept load, less reliance on visuals, longer sentences, and more literary language.

Level 4 builds reading stamina by providing more text per page, increased use of punctuation, greater variation in sentence patterns, and increasingly challenging vocabulary.

Level 5 encourages children to move from "learning to read" to "reading to learn" by providing even more text, varied writing styles, and less familiar topics.

Whichever book is right for your reader, Blastoff! Readers are the perfect books to build confidence and encourage a love of reading that will last a lifetime!

This edition first published in 2019 by Bellwether Media, Inc.

No part of this publication may be reproduced in whole or in part without written permission of the publisher. For information regarding permission, write to Bellwether Media, Inc., Attention: Permissions Department, 6012 Blue Circle Drive, Minnetonka, MN 55343.

Library of Congress Cataloging-in-Publication Data

Names: Noll, Elizabeth, author.
Title: Coding in Your School / by Elizabeth Noll.
Description: Minneapolis, MN : Bellwether Media, Inc., [2019] | Series: Blastoff! Readers. Coding Is Everywhere | Includes bibliographical references and index. | Audience: Kindergarten through third grade.
Identifiers: LCCN 2017060021 (print) | LCCN 2017061777 (ebook) | ISBN 9781626178380 (hardcover : alk. paper) | ISBN 9781618914828 (pbk. : alk. paper) | ISBN 9781681035796 (ebook)
Subjects: LCSH: Computer programming–Juvenile literature. | Education, Elementary–Activity programs–Juvenile literature.
Classification: LCC QA76.6115 (ebook) | LCC QA76.6115 .N65 2019 (print) | DDC 005.1–dc23
LC record available at https://lccn.loc.gov/2017060021

Editor: Christina Leaf   Designer: Brittany McIntosh

Printed in the United States of America, North Mankato, MN

Table of Contents

Coding in Your School

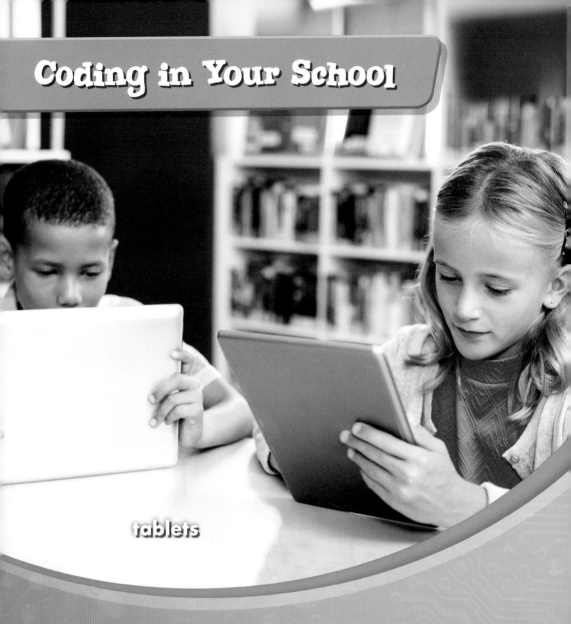

tablets

Where are the computers in your school? Do you have a media center? Do you use a **tablet**?

Computers are everywhere!

How do computers work? They follow instructions called **code**.

Scratch

Code directs everything on computers.
People write code with special
programming languages.

In school, computers
and web sites use code.
Calculators use code, too.

Even punching in your lunch number uses code!

The History of Coding in Schools

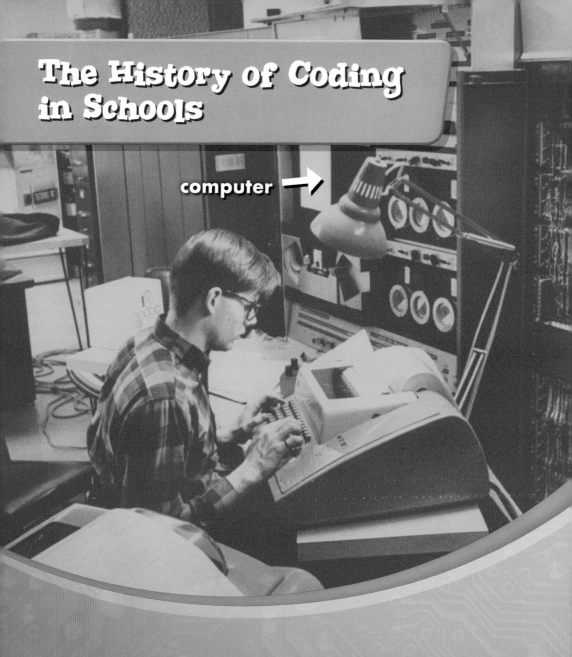

computer ➛

In the 1960s, computers took up a whole room. Code was written on paper cards.

Some schools had these. Others had computer **terminals**.

terminal

code

By the 1970s and 1980s, computers were smaller and more powerful.

Many schools had computer labs. Students started to learn **programming**.

Today, most schools have computers. Media centers have laptops or tablets.

Teachers use **smart boards**. Students do research and homework online.

How Does Coding Work in Your School?

Many classroom activities depend on coding. Code tells the computer where to send your online homework.

It creates the web sites that you use for your **biography** report.

Code even helps you check out
library books! Each book has a
barcode. The code in the scanner
reads these. It connects each
barcode to the right book title.

Check Out a Library Book

look up book and get it from a shelf

spell the title wrong, cannot find the book

give librarian your library card

forget library card, cannot check out

scan book

check out!

New **technologies** make school easier for kids who learn in different ways.

Code helps students practice reading, math, and more! What code can you create?

Glossary

biography—a history of a person's life

code—instructions for a computer

programming—writing code for computers

programming languages—special languages that humans use to talk to computers

smart boards—interactive white boards that are computers

tablet—a handheld computer with a touch screen instead of a keyboard

technologies—tools created by using science

terminals—machines with keyboards and monitors that connect to a larger computer somewhere else

To Learn More

AT THE LIBRARY

Kelly, James Floyd. *The Story of Coding.* New York, N.Y.: DK Publishing, 2017.

Lyons, Heather, and Elizabeth Tweedale. *Learn to Program.* Minneapolis, Minn.: Lerner Publications, 2017.

Wainewright, Max. *How to Code: A Step-by-Step Guide to Computer Coding.* New York, N.Y.: Sterling Children's Books, 2016.

ON THE WEB

Learning more about coding in your school is as easy as 1, 2, 3.

1. Go to www.factsurfer.com.

2. Enter "coding in your school" into the search box.

3. Click the "Surf" button and you will see a list of related web sites.

With factsurfer.com, finding more information is just a click away.

Index